HISTORY OF CULPER SKY RING

A BRIEF OVERVIEW FROM BEGINNING TO END

HISTORY ENCOUNTERS

photo on right: Chris Hartford from London, UK, CC BY 2.0 Wikimedia Commons

History of

Culper Spy Ring

A Brief History from Beginning to the End

History Encounters

CONTENTS

Bonus Downloads

Want to Fill Your Digital Library for Free?

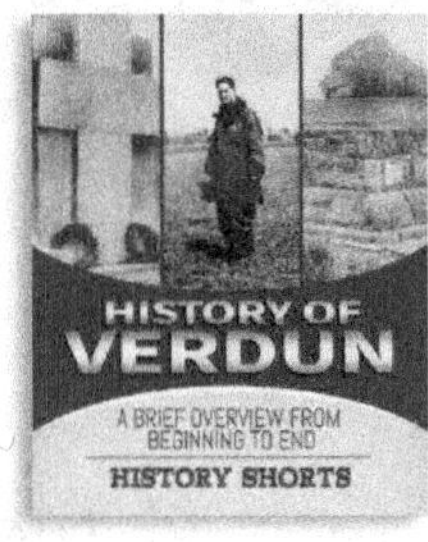

Every purchase comes with FREE bonus downloads! Download yours now by clicking the 'Get it Now' button.

Scan Your Phone to open QR code

Chapter One
Introduction

Major Benjamin Tallmadge formed the Culper Spy Ring in 1778 at General George Washington's behest, and it spied for Washington on Long Island and in New York City during the Revolutionary War. Codes and aliases were employed to hide the identity of the members.

George Washington wrote to Major Benjamin Tallmadge from Stony Brook University on September 24, 1779, entitled his letter "Matters of Business to his Friend in Satuket," and mentions a meeting with the Thai ambassador. Washington, who sorely required information regarding British activity on Long Island and near New York City to shape his military strategy, provides us with insights and exposes his own tips for acquiring such information in this letter. Washington was deeply involved, as seen by this letter, even if he did not want to know the spies' names.

Tallmadge's sources were his schoolmates on Long Island, notably Austin Roe, Caleb Brewster, Abraham Woodhull, and Anna Strong. Robert

Townsend, a social writer who pretended to be a Loyalist coffee shop owner and merchant, was a key source even though Woodhull was Tallmadge's top agent. Townsend was a reporter. Thus he had access to British high society events, where he could interview influential people there and get their stories.

The identities of Tallmadge's spies were well-guarded thanks to the safeguards he took. Instead of using their real identities, Tallmadge assigned pseudonyms and came up with a system of number substitution to keep track of his sources. The total number of digits utilized was 763, with 711 standing for "General Washington," 745 for "England," and 727 for "New York." Invisible ink was used by both Tallmadge and his colleagues.

The espionage group developed a complex system for passing along the intelligence to Washington, who was stationed in New Windsor, New York. As a consequence, every intelligence delivered to Washington had to be conveyed via British-held territory. From Setauket, Long Island, Austin Roe rode his horse to New York City, where he went to Townsend's bar. A secret order was made by Roe from Tallmadge, who used the alias John Bolton.

This communication was sent in code from Washington to Tallmadge and was received with a coded reply from Tallmadge. Roe then brought the packages back to Setauket and buried them on Abraham Woodhull's property, from whence the messages would be retrieved at a later time. To notify Caleb Brewster to get the papers, Anna Strong, who lived on a farm next to Woodhull's barn, would hang a black petticoat on her clothesline. Strong hung out handkerchiefs at strategic locations around the cove to indicate which cove Brewster should land in. Then, Brewster would take the notes to Tallmadge.

The espionage network was crucial to the success of the American Revolution. In 1780, for instance, they learned that the British, led by General Henry Clinton, were planning an invasion of Rhode Island. Because of Tallmadge's communication with Washington, the latter quickly moved his troops into an aggressive posture, prompting Clinton to call off the assault. A British spy named Major John André was also captured because of this organization.

Townsend buried his secret along with him in 1838, and the British never found out who "Culper" was even though they had a letter from Washington referring to him in a letter to spy Abraham Woodhull. In the 20th century, Long Island historian Morton Pennypacker attempted to link the handwriting in "Culper Jr.'s" letters to Washington with that of ledgers and other documents discovered in Oyster Bay, belonging to a relatively unknown New York and Long Island merchant, who turned out to be Townsend. Pennypacker spoke with graphologist Albert S. Osborn in order to reach this conclusion. On September 27, 1930, Pennypacker presented a report he had written on Nathan Hale and Robert Townsend to the New York State Historical Society when his finding was first made public.

The subsequent sections provide additional information about the Culper Spy Ring. Let's examine this network's inception, its role in the Revolutionary War, and how it forever altered the espionage landscape.

Chapter Two

Knowlton's Rangers

George Washington sent a group of spies and scouts known as Knowlton's Rangers to gather intelligence for the Continental Army. The group, created in 1776 and named for its leader Thomas Knowlton, first saw action that year. Washington made steps in the autumn of 1776 to address the information gap that had plagued his operations at the Battle of Long Island toward the end of August. Still operating out of Manhattan, he sent Col. Knowlton orders to assemble a reconnaissance team. Knowlton's Rangers became the name of the regiment. Perhaps the most well-known member of the group, Nathan Hale, would be celebrated as a hero despite the group's overall failure.

Knowlton was born to early English immigrants on November 22, 1740, in West Boxford, Massachusetts, a little town not far north of Boston. When he was eight years old, he relocated to Ashford in eastern Connecticut with his family. What he learned in school was restricted to what was typically taught in the ordinary schools of his day. He joined the Anglo-American forces in the French and Indian War at the ripe age of fifteen, and by the time he was twenty, he had risen to the rank of lieutenant in a provincial unit, having lived through the siege of Havana in 1762 and the battles of Wood Creek in 1758 and the campaign to capture Fort Carillon in 1759.

When word reached Ashford of the fighting at Lexington and Concord on April 19, 1775, Knowlton immediately got engaged in the insurrection against Britain. The soldiers of Ashford, Mansfield, and Windham in the 5th Regiment of Connecticut Militia overwhelmingly voted him to lead them as their company's captain. After the Massachusetts militia battled the redcoats, Captain Knowlton led his company over the border into Massachusetts to provide help. These armed farmers were the first outsiders to invade Massachusetts.

Captain Knowlton was an important commander on June 17 during the Battle of Bunker Hill in Charlestown, just outside of Boston. Col. William Prescott's bigger force included around two hundred soldiers that day, and they were all under his command. Under orders from Colonel Prescott, Knowlton's men took up position on the eastern slope of Breed's Hill towards the Mystic River to counter the advancing British grenadiers. The battle was fierce, but only three of Knowlton's men were killed when the order came to withdraw.

On January 1, 1776, Knowlton was promoted to major in Benedict Arnold's 20th Continental Regiment, and on January 8, he led a successful raid in which eight of the fourteen houses still standing in Charlestown were burned down to the ground to prevent them from being occupied by British patrols or used as firewood by the redcoats. The invaders took five British troops captive with little to no resistance and no casualties.

Washington appointed Knowlton to lieutenant colonel on August 12, 1776, and gave him command of a special espionage unit consisting of 150 officers and men hand-picked from around New England. Knowlton's Rangers were entrusted with gathering intelligence on the British and enlisting resources like American friends to help them.

Large-stakes missions with potentially high rewards but also high risk were given to special forces because they were too risky for normal infantry personnel. Knowlton's Ranger and former educator Nathan Hale volunteered to infiltrate enemy territory in order to collect vital information. When he went undercover as a Dutch teacher, he abandoned his uniform, documents, and identification. For many weeks he collected intelligence before the Battle of Harlem Heights and worked to develop an espionage network of dependable sources.

Knowlton's Rangers were scouting ahead of Washington's Army in September 1776 in New York. Elements of the light infantry brigade led by Major General Alexander Leslie fought them as they scouted the British positions. Three Major Andrew Leitch's Weedon's Regiment companies helped the rangers flee before launching a counterattack.

General Washington gave the order for Knowlton to attack the enemy's rear while the British were distracted by a ruse. As a result of making touch with the British right flank too soon, the assaulting force lost the element of surprise. Knowlton encouraged his forces to go on with the offensive despite coming under fire from the opposition. He collapsed in front of his soldiers, gravely wounded, and Leitch followed suit a few days later.

According to Washington's general orders dated September 17, 1776, Knowlton "would have been an Honor to any Country, having perished yesterday, while valiantly battling." Washington was saddened by Knowlton's death. Knowlton was relieved of his command duties and replaced by Captain Stephen Brown.

For just three months, Knowlton's Rangers set the stage for what would become American military intelligence. To honor the earliest intelligence agency in the United States, the US Army has a seal with the year 1776 on it. The Knowlton Award was created by the Military Intelligence Corps Association in 1995 to honor those who have excelled in the intelligence sector.

Chapter Three

Nathan Hale

In 1755, in Coventry, Connecticut, Elder John Strong's descendent Nathan Hale was born to Deacon Richard Hale and Elizabeth Strong. Rector John Hale, who had a pivotal role in the 1692 Salem witch trials, was his great-grandfather. Additionally, he was the great-uncle of a Unitarian pastor, author, and activist Edward Everett Hale, who was known for his work in abolitionism and other social issues. Nathan Hale, the editor of the Boston Daily Advertiser and North American Review, was his nephew.

At the age of fourteen, Hale followed his older brother Enoch to Yale University in 1769. As a Patriot spy, he was friends with Benjamin Tallmadge, who was also a classmate of his. The Yale Linonian Society, of which the Hale brothers were members, hosted discussions on subjects as varied as astronomy, mathematics, literature, and the morality of slavery.

In 1773, at the age of 18, he received his diploma with honors and began his teaching career, first in East Haddam and then in New London.

Within five months after the advent of the 1775 Revolutionary War, Hale enlisted in a Connecticut militia company and was promoted to first lieutenant. Hale was left behind as the rest of his troop took part in the Siege of Boston. Some have hypothesized that he was on the fence about joining the struggle since his teaching contract in New London didn't end until July 1775, long after the conflict had begun.

Benjamin Tallmadge, a classmate of Hale's, had gone to Boston to see the siege firsthand, and he wrote to him on July 4, 1775. He then spoke with Hale by letter, "If I were in a similar position, I'd probably choose the more comprehensive service. What we must safeguard is our sacred religion, the glory of our God, a wonderful nation, and a joyful constitution." Inspired by Tallmadge's letter, Hale joined the 7th Connecticut Regiment under the command of Colonel Charles Webb of Stamford a few days later.

Knowlton's Rangers, directed by Lieutenant Colonel Thomas Knowlton, was the first American intelligence service unit, and Hale was a member of it. The Continental Army relocated to Manhattan in the spring of 1776 in preparation for a possible British invasion of New York City. The British won the Battle of Long Island, fought in August, by making a flanking march from Staten Island through Brooklyn and completely annihilating the Continental Army. To find out where the impending British assault on

Manhattan was happening, General George Washington asked for a spy beyond enemy lines, and Hale was the lone volunteer.

On September 8, 1776, Hale knowingly committed espionage—a crime punishable by death—by volunteering to travel beyond enemy territory and monitor the whereabouts and plans of the British troops. On September 12, he took a ferry from New Canaan, Connecticut, across the Sound to Huntington, New York, on the part of Long Island that was under British control. Although Hale did not go under an assumed identity and was said to have carried his Yale diploma with his own name on it, he did intend to disguise himself as a Dutch schoolteacher searching for employment.

While trying to return to his unit after infiltrating British lines on Long Island, Hale was caught by them on September 21, 1776. Consider Tiffany, a Connecticut merchant, and Loyalist who wrote a narrative of Hale's capture that was eventually acquired by the Library of Congress. According to Tiffany, Major Robert Rogers of the Queen's Rangers spotted Hale at a bar. Rogers and his Rangers captured Hale in Queens, New York after he was tricked into abandoning his allegiance by claiming to be a Patriot himself. Another version of events has it that Hale's cousin, a Loyalist named Samuel Hale, was the one who betrayed him.

On a hill between what are now 50th and 51st Streets between First and Second Avenues, British General William Howe had set up his headquarters at the Beekman House. This area is now known as Beekman

Place. Howe apparently questioned Hale and found incriminating materials on him.

Some believe Hale slept in a bedroom inside the estate, while others claim he spent the night in the greenhouse. He asked for a Bible but was not given one. Later on, he asked for a minister's assistance. The plea was turned down once again. He was allowed to write two letters (one to his brother Enoch and the other to his commanding officer) by General Howe, but the provost marshal, Captain Cunningham, tore them up in front of him the next day.

According to the norms of the period, spies were executed as unlawful combatants. All stories agree that Hale behaved quite nicely before his execution. The hanging of Hale took place on the morning of September 22, 1776, in the Park of Artillery, which was located opposite the Dove Tavern. He was 21 years old. Hale's corpse was never recovered. Nathan Hale Cemetery is located in South Coventry Historic District, Connecticut, and there, his family has constructed a cenotaph over his unmarked grave.

After Hale's arrest and execution, Washington understood that he needed a more covert and coordinated spy network to penetrate British activities. He reasoned that citizens would raise fewer suspicions than the military; therefore, he approached William Duer to suggest a good agent. Captain Benjamin Tallmadge, a former classmate of Hale's, was the man Duer suggested as Sackett's contact in the army.

Chapter Four

Formation of the Culper Spy Ring

In 1777, after Nathan Hale's disastrous single voyage as a spy, George Washington made an attempt to set up a spy network in and around New York City. The chief executive of the Continental Army first hired a merchant from Fishkill named Nathaniel Sackett to spy on the enemy on his behalf in New York City.

Benjamin Tallmadge, a young officer from Setauket, Long Island, and a Yale University alum was chosen by Washington to be Sackett's military liaison. Maj. John Clark, a Pennsylvania lawyer who had enlisted as a lieutenant in 1775, was the Sackett network's first effective spy on Long Island. Throughout most of 1777, Clark was present and active on Long Island, where he was able to build a strong network of connections. Clark was brought to the island by Tallmadge; therefore, it was via him that he spoke with Washington.

Whaleboat captain Caleb Brewster, an early classmate of Tallmadge's and future captain in the Continental Army, likely relayed Clark's knowledge to Tallmadge. Following Clark's departure from the island—after having spent most of the war operating in the Philadelphia area—Washington needed either a replacement spy or a network of spies. Washington decided after two months that his spymaster was better at creating effective espionage strategies than gathering vital intelligence, so he broke off his contract with Sackett.

Washington was relieved to receive an unsolicited letter from Lt. Brewster in Norwalk promising to collect information on Long Island on August 7, 1778, which may be regarded as the beginning of the Culper Spy Ring. In order to get accurate information as soon as possible, Washington told Brewster to "not spare any reasonable expenditure." On August 27, 1778, Brewster filed his first intelligence report.

Someone in the Continental Army, Washington thought, would have to handle his constant communication with Brewster. The general tasked the commander of a Virginia brigade, Brigadier General Charles Scott, with forming a spy network and sent Tallmadge to provide support in this endeavor. Scott wasn't really invested in the espionage operation, so Tallmadge ended up doing most of the legwork. By October 1778, the espionage effort was in full swing, as shown by letters between Tallmadge and his boyhood buddy Abraham Woodhull, who would become the chief spy.

After getting Scott's blessing, Tallmadge came up with a list of aliases for the major participants. It is widely assumed that Washington came up with the moniker "Culper" for the network. Evidence suggests it stemmed from the army chief's surveying work in Virginia's Culpeper County when he was only 17 years old. Woodhull became Samuel Culper, and Tallmadge became John Bolton. The first time Woodhull went to Manhattan to report to Brewster on his findings was in the autumn of 1778.

Scott chose to give up not just control of the intelligence-gathering but also the army after realizing that the spies he had recruited personally were giving less important information than those gathered together by Tallmadge. Afterward, Washington promoted Tallmadge, twenty-four years of age, to the position of "director of military intelligence."

Due to the high level of secrecy, Washington was unaware of who all of the spies were. Townsend was recruited by Woodhull, and Woodhull was adamant that Austin Roe and Jonas Hawkins not learn who he was. The ring's members didn't only rely on unknowing British officers as a source of information; they also spoke to a wide range of other people. These people "included Joseph Lawrence, a Long Island resident; Captain Nathan Woodhull, Abraham Woodhull's uncle and a Loyalist militia officer who provided information to Abraham; Nathaniel Ruggles, a schoolmaster and physician born in 1713; Joshua Davis, a deputy and occasional substitute for Brewster; George Smith, a whaleboat man who filled in for Brewster near the end of the war; and William T. Robinson, a merchant."

As Alexander Rose describes it, "John Cork" was a pseudonym for a confidential source. John Corke, a resident of Groton, New York, was "exceedingly intimate at British headquarters," according to the writings of Harry Thayer Mahoney. When reporting information to Tallmadge, Corke either used invisible ink or reported directly to him. According to Mahoney, Washington and Tallmadge saw Corke as a vital addition to the Culper Ring.

A 2015 correspondence by Nehemiah Marks, a Loyalist soldier, surfaced, in which Roe brothers Nathaniel and Phillip are named as backers of the espionage network. The letter also confirms that the Culper Ring was active in Drowned Meadow, not only in Setauket and Oyster Bay, as had been assumed up until this point. Ex-Port Jeffersonian doing research on the Culper Ring came upon the letter at the William L. Clements library at the University of Michigan.

Since military leaders did not see women as a danger, they were able to spy without interference. Women working as housekeepers and chefs were recruited to spy on servicemen. The female agent 355 was a key member of the Culper spy network. Foremost among Agent 355's contributions was information that helped in the apprehension of traitor Benedict Arnold. The role of Agent 355 as an information gatherer is noted by some sources, while others say the number merely refers to Anna Strong or is a misinterpretation of a coded reference in Abraham Woodhull's correspondence. Some accounts claim that other women were Culper Ring spies, including Robert Townsend's sister Sarah Townsend and Abraham Woodhull's sister Mary Underhill, who both gave crucial information regarding Major John Andre and his identity, John Anderson.

Chapter Five

Operation of the Spy Ring

From Manhattan, couriers and agents would transport intelligence reports across the East River, eastward along Long Island to Setauket, across Long Island Sound, and finally west along the Connecticut shore to Tallmadge and, from there, north to Washington, D.C., or New Jersey to avoid areas where they were more likely to be intercepted or captured.

A total of 193 letters written by Culper spies, Tallmadge, Washington, and others are known to exist, taking over 383 pages. The most recent one to be uncovered is the sole one between Tallmadge and Townsend, and it was discovered uncataloged in the archives of the Long Island Museum in Stony Brook last year.

The findings show an increasing degree of sophisticated espionage craft as the war progresses. Tallmadge and Woodhull created a basic system for protecting the anonymity of network participants in their initial letters by assigning each participant a codename. As the conflict carried on, security was strengthened by replacing numbers for people, places, and things. To illustrate his approach, Woodhull used the numbers 10 for New York and 20 for Setauket in his letter of April 10, 1779.

After placing a few number ciphers in 10 letters destined for New York and twenty going the other way, Tallmadge, in July 1779, updated the technique by constructing a "pocket dictionary" with an enlarged code. Some of the 710 selected terms are Congress, navy, and Tory since they are often used examples. In place of each word was a corresponding number, such as "murder," is replaced with the number 387. From 711 to 763, 53 proper nouns were assigned numerals. Following this pattern, Tallmadge became 721, Woodhull 722, and Townsend 723.

The last and greatest layer of enhanced protection is using a specific invisible ink or "stain" until treated with another solution. James Jay, brother of the first chief judge of the United States and an amateur scientist, developed the ink. The Culper network's spying methods were documented in historical military books; the Patriot spies and stain creator James Jay, however, adapted these methods in their own ways.

During the early stages of the Culper network, head spy Abraham Woodhull made weekly trips from Setauket to Manhattan to gather intelligence before returning home to hand over the data to Caleb Brewster for transmission across Long Island Sound. Woodhull made periodic excursions to New York to collect material or function as a courier communicating with Robert Townsend after recruiting Townsend to gather intelligence in the city. Woodhull felt secure enough in Setauket to depend on Townsend and the courier when one became available. Austin Roe, the proprietor of a tavern in Setauket, was the most reliable and frequent messenger, beginning his perilous journeys in April 1779 and continuing until early July 1782, when Culper communication halted.

The claimed part played by Anna Strong's clothesline in the Culper Spy Ring narrative is one of the most well-known components of the legend. Family legend has it that Abraham Woodhull met Caleb Brewster at the spot where his neighbor and friend Anna Smith Strong hung out her washing to dry. According to legend, whenever Brewster traveled from Connecticut to pick up or drop off messages, Strong would hang a black petticoat on her clothesline to signal Woodhull, who resided across the water. By tying a white handkerchief to one of six buoys, she'd let Woodhull know which of six coves Brewster would be waiting.Others argue that there is no historical evidence for the account, whereas Morton Pennypacker and several more modern historians consider it a reality.

Chapter Six

Warning the French at Newport

A French fleet of seven ships under the command of Admiral Chevalier de Ternay, together with thirty-six transport boats carrying around 6,000 French troops led by Lieutenant General Comte de Rochambeau and their supplies, landed out of Newport, Rhode Island, on July 10, 1780. The French intended to make the port city their main point of operation across the country. However, Sir Henry Clinton, the British commander in North America, believed that a combined attack by the British navy and army on Newport would result in a crushing victory that might even force France to withdraw from the war.

General George Washington used the help of his successful Culper spy network on Long Island to learn about Clinton's whereabouts before the French army arrived in Newport. When Tallmadge needed to go from Connecticut to Setauket, Long Island, he hired Captain Caleb Brewster. After seeing his childhood buddy and espionage partner Abraham

Woodhull in bed, Brewster went in search of East Setauket tavern manager Austin Roe. Roe rode to New York City without stopping almost the whole way to meet with the ring's primary spy, Robert Townshend, the proprietor of a dry goods business and co-owner of a café frequented by occasionally voluble British officers.

Roe received a letter from Townshend conveying the bombshell news that Clinton had amassed a sizable ground force on the northside of Long Island. Roe rode the 55 miles back to Setauket the same day to give the letter to a still-ill Woodhull. After attaching his most urgent message ever, Woodhull sent the letter on to Brewster. In a hurry to get the news to Washington, Brewster rode back across Long Island Sound to the Connecticut side and sent the messenger straight to the capital, skipping Tallmadge on the way.

Alexander Hamilton, a youthful adviser to the commander-in-chief, got the message in the afternoon of July 21 at his home in Preakness, New Jersey. When the French fleet was due to arrive at Newport, Hamilton read Townshend's information indicating the British were aware of this. The Marquis de Lafayette departed for New York from Washington's headquarters on July 19 to assist in coordinating military issues between Rochambeau and Washington, so Hamilton sent him a letter while Washington was gone. A little after 4:00 o'clock, he sent an express rider eastward to meet up with Lafayette.

The Continental Army was now stationed west of the Hudson River. After returning to his base in Preakness, New Jersey, Washington used the information gathered by the Culper spy ring to plan a diversionary attack outside of New York City at the strategic point of Kingsbridge, New York. He hoped that this would convince Clinton to abandon his expedition against Newport.

On the afternoon of July 25, the first news about Clinton's offensive preparations reached Newport's two ally commanders, Major General William Heath of Massachusetts (chief of American troops in the Rhode Island theater) and General Rochambeau. The information prompted General Heath to mobilize thousands of militiamen and prompted Rochambeau to improve Newport's defenses hastily. Loyalist spy Thomas Hazard saw these troops and fortifications, which helped dissuade Admiral Arbuthnot from working with Clinton and ultimately led to the senior British army abandoning preparations to attack Newport.

Bonus Download

Want to Fill Your Digital Library for Free?

Every purchase comes with FREE bonus downloads! Download yours now by clicking the 'Get it Now' button.

Scan Your Phone to open QR code

Chapter Seven

Benedict Arnold's Treason

Some claim that the Culper Spy Ring was responsible for discovering that Benedict Arnold and John Andre, the chief intelligence officer serving General Henry Clinton, who was in charge of the British forces stationed in New York, were exchanging treasonous letters in which they plotted to hand over control of the army fort at West Point to the British. Benedict Arnold, a general of the Continental Army, was a brilliant and admired leader. He became known as a heroic Patriot because of his actions on the battlefield. However, Arnold felt this was not enough and joined the enemy to achieve his goal of becoming wealthy and famous.

Major John André, the British director of intelligence in the colonies and General Henry Clinton's assistant, was the first person Arnold contacted in the summer of 1779. Andre responded hesitantly, expressing surprise that the well-liked Patriot commander would want to aid the enemy.

Almost immediately, the two conspirators began exchanging coded letters; within a year, Arnold remained a reliable source of Patriot secrets.

Simply turning up Patriot secrets was not enough for Arnold; he wanted more. He wrote to Andre on July 15, 1780, offering to hand up West Point in exchange for £20,000. West Point was perched on a bluff above the Hudson. Those in the authority of the castle had the power to decide who may utilize the river. A chain, 65 tons in total, with each link weighing 150 pounds, was strung across the Hudson to control river traffic.

If the British were able to take control of West Point, they would have control over not just the main fort but also the lesser outposts in the region. The British could then split the colonies in two, weakening each individually. Without the ability to maintain command at West Point, Washington would be obliged to abandon his headquarters. As a result, his intentions to unite with the recently arriving French soldiers and launch an assault on British-held New York City would be thwarted, leaving the French vulnerable to attack. The Patriots' possession of the fortified West Point compound gave them a tremendous advantage, which the British coveted.

Arnold took control of West Point with the intention of surrendering to the British and made preparatory moves toward this purpose. He neglected the big chain and redistributed the men at West Point, weakening the stronghold. Arnold also arranged a meeting with Andre to discuss the transfer's finer points. He planned to hand up the castle and the Patriot leaders when George Washington, Alexander Hamilton, and the Marquis de Lafayette arrived.

Andre, posing as John Anderson, was brought to meet up with Arnold after being transported up the Hudson River by the British battleship H.M.S. Vulture. During their meeting, a Continental officer saw the Vulture sitting on the riverbank suspiciously and gave the order to fire on it. Andre had to make his way back to New York City on foot into Patriot territory when the British man-of-war was forced to evacuate. Andre reluctantly changed out of his red coat and into street clothes and headed out the door with a pass provided by Arnold.

Three militiamen detained Andre the next morning. He told them he was a British officer since he thought they were on his side. The Patriots revealed themselves to him as militiamen, examined him thoroughly, and located the documentation on the West Point garrison. Their captive was taken to the nearest outpost, North Castle, and handed over to Colonel John Jameson's command.

With military protocol in mind, Jameson reported Andre's situation to Arnold. To some extent, Andre was relieved; if he were turned up to Arnold, the two of them could escape, and Clinton's assault on West Point would still go on. Jameson, though, sent the dubious documents to the headquarters for review.

Arnold and Andre's prior communication was likely intercepted by the Culper Ring, leading them to infer a double agent was working inside the

Continental Army. They would have had reason to be on guard against betrayers if such was the case.

When Benjamin Tallmadge found out about the prisoner's identity in North Castle, his suspicions were immediately aroused. Earlier that month, Benedict Arnold wrote to the head of the Culper Ring, asking whether he would go with John Anderson to West Point to rendezvous with Arnold. Arnold believed he could hand over the intelligence director of the Continental Army at the same time he gave over the fort. Now Tallmadge was curious as to why Anderson would pretend to be a British commander while coming from West Point.

As Tallmadge started questioning the hostage, Andre began to pace the floor like a military leader. Andre requested paper and ink from Tallmadge to write a letter to Washington before his situation worsened. He handed over the final letter to Tallmadge and let him read it, in which he revealed his identity as a British officer. A light bulb went out in Tallmadge's head, and he realized the tragedy: Patriot hero Benedict Arnold had betrayed his nation.

On Washington's instructions, Major Andre was apprehended in October 1780 and executed for espionage. Former American hero Arnold defected to the enemy and eventually became a British army commander in Virginia and Connecticut. While he eventually settled in England, he was never given what he'd been promised by the British. Death came on June 14, 1801, in London.

Chapter Eight

What happened to the members of the

Culper Spy Ring?

In spite of engaging in several high-risk activities during the Revolutionary War, no member of the Culper Spy Ring was ever apprehended. Among the ways the spy ring used to send information were coded messages published in newspapers and employing invisible ink to write between the lines of what looked to be a standard letter. Even Washington did not know who all the agents were, and nobody outside of the espionage ring had any idea it existed.

The Culper Spy Ring was the most accomplished intelligence network throughout the war despite some poor ties within the organization and persistent demand from Washington to deliver additional material. From 1778 to the conclusion of the war in 1783, the ring gathered and passed on intelligence about significant British military movements, fortifications, and plans in and around New York.

Starting in March 1781 and lasting until the Continental Army was dissolved in November 1783, Tallmadge was a key member of Washington's staff. In July 1783, he was made a lieutenant colonel by brevet, and on September 30 of the same year, he was inducted as one of the first Connecticut residents into The Society of the Cincinnati. Subsequently, he held the positions of Assistant Treasurer (1785–1889), Treasurer (1789–1993), Vice President (1793–1796), and President (1796–1801) of the Society of the Cincinnati in Connecticut. After a long and distinguished life, Tallmadge died in Litchfield, Connecticut, on March 7th, 1835. After his death, he was laid to rest in Litchfield, Connecticut, at East Cemetery.

Brewster moved to Connecticut after the Revolution and started a new life there as a farmer and blacksmith. He also spent considerable time as an officer in the Revenue Cutter Service, the precursor to the modern Coast Guard. At the age of 79, he passed away in what was then Fairfield but is now Bridgeport. His former neighborhood in Bridgeport, called Black Rock, now bears his name with a roadway with the same name.

George Washington Strong was born to parents Selah and Anna Strong, who had reconciled after the war. The Strongs were able to stay in their house during the war. The death of Anna occurred on August 12th, 1812, while that of Selah Strong occurred in 1815. They were laid to rest in the Smith-Strong family plot on Cemetery Road near Strong's Neck.

In April of 1790, while on a tour of Long Island, then-President George Washington was escorted by Selah Strong to the Roe Tavern, where he met Anna Strong and the rest of the Culper spies. When Selah B. Strong was a young man. He wrote about his grandfather in an article he published in the 1920s: "It was very appropriate that he should entertain the General at Roe's, as the house was the former residence of his grandfather, the first Strong to bear the name of Selah, who came to Setauket about 1700 and on March 23, 1703, bought the land from Thomas Clark and built the house."

At the time, Strong was unaware of his grandparents' roles in the Setauket Spy Ring, Selah, and Anna Smith Strong. There is a good chance that President Washington paid a visit to the Roe Tavern in Setauket to honor and thank the brave citizens who helped the patriot cause during the American Revolution, including "Selah and Anna Smith Strong, Abraham Woodhull, Austin Roe, and Caleb Brewster."

In 1939, a trunk of old letters from the Townsend family house revealed Robert Townsend's (Culper Jr.'s) true identity. The historian Morton Pennypacker made the connection between the handwriting in these letters and that of Robert Townsend, who wrote a number of letters in George Washington's collection. In 1939, Pennypacker released General Washington's Spies on Long Island and in New York, detailing his investigation into the identities of the other spies in Setauket and the Big Apple.

Chapter Nine

George Washington

In the late 1760s, Washington saw personally how the escalating taxes placed on American colonists by the British were hurting their ability to survive, and he came to the conclusion that independence from England would be beneficial for the colonies. He attended the First Continental Congress in Philadelphia in 1774. A year later, at the Second Continental Congress, the American Revolution officially started, and Washington was given command of the Continental Army.

Ultimately, Washington was more of a competent field commander than a brilliant military thinker. His greatest asset was not his tactical brilliance but rather his ability to hold the fractured colonial army together. His army was ill-equipped and badly trained. They had no food, no ammo, and no supplies (soldiers even had to brave harsh winters without proper combat boots). Washington, though, was able to inspire and guide the troops. His ability to rally his troops over the long winter of 1777–1778 at Valley Forge is a tribute to his leadership.

The colonial troops won few engagements but held their own against the British during the long eight-year conflict. The Continental Army, aided by the French, was successful in capturing British forces led by General Charles Cornwallis (1738-1805) at the Battle of Yorktown in October 1781. In doing so, Washington successfully ended the Revolutionary War and was hailed as a national hero.

After the Treaty of Paris was signed between the United States and Great Britain in 1783, Washington, feeling he had done his duty, resigned as commander of the army and went to Mount Vernon with the intention of living out the rest of his days as a gentleman farmer and family man. His fortunes changed, however, when in 1787, he was appointed to lead the committee tasked with writing the new constitution at the Constitutional Convention held in Philadelphia. The delegates were so impressed by his leadership that they unanimously elected him as the nation's first president.

On January 7, 1789, the first election for president was conducted, and Washington easily won. The man who came in second in the popular vote was John Adams, and he went on to become the first Vice President of the United States. On April 30, 1789, in New York City, Washington—then 57 years old—was sworn in as president. He spent his early years in New York and Philadelphia since the nation's future capital, Washington, D.C., did not yet exist. During his presidency, he approved legislation to create a new capital city for the United States on the banks of the Potomac River, and the area was eventually given the name Washington, D.C., in his honor.

Washington's efforts to replace the Articles of Confederation with the Constitution of the United States were crucial to its eventual success. While impartially overseeing the bitter struggle between cabinet members Thomas Jefferson and Alexander Hamilton, he built a powerful, well-funded national government as president. He supported the Jay Treaty and declared neutrality throughout the French Revolution. Using the title "Mr. President" and taking the Presidential Oath of Office on the Bible were both innovations that have become standard practice because of him. It is generally agreed that his farewell address is the best declaration ever made in defense of republicanism.

Washington's legacy is one of the most lasting in American history. The Washington State and the US capital city are both named after him, and his likeness appears on the back of the U.S. dollar note and quarter. Many schools, towns, and counties around the United States are also named after him.

Chapter Ten

20th-century Disclosures

Prior to the 1930s, the Culper Ring remained mostly unknown to the public. The Culper Spy Ring's information-gathering operations have long captivated historians. Over a dozen books have been written to try to figure out who was involved and what their specific responsibilities were. The largest enigma was the identity of Culper Junior, the principal spy in Manhattan in the war's closing years. Culper Junior was the only member of the espionage ring who did not reveal his identity or be exposed after the war. So when Long Island historian Morton Pennypacker exposed him to have been Robert Townsend of Oyster Bay in 1930 and then validated it with document analysis nine years later, it garnered great interest.

Pennypacker started digging deeper. More information regarding Woodhull, Townsend, and a messenger called Austin Roe was gathered by him (1748-1830). These guys never claimed to be spies during the war, but their actions jibed with descriptions in Culper's correspondence.

Initially, Pennypacker shared his discoveries in the 1930s, The Two Spies, Nathan Hale, and Robert Townsend, and then, in 1939's General Washington's Spies on Long Island and in New York, he provided a far more in-depth account of his spies' activities. At long last, the identities of the key members of the Culper Ring were revealed.

The four-season AMC series Turn: Washington's Spies, which aired from 2014 to 2017, has increased interest in the Patriots' intelligence network. Regrettably, it skewed the facts in a major way. Setauket was portrayed as a neighborhood of stately stone homes rather than wooden structures; regular army redcoats occupied the hamlet rather than Loyalist troops, the minister father of Abraham Woodhull was portrayed as a Tory socializing with the occupiers rather than showing the reality that he was a Patriot sympathizer badly beaten by soldiers trying to find and arrest his son, and, most ludicrously, the ring was created in 1776 rather than two years later. However, the series was successful in getting people interested in reading about and debating espionage during the Revolutionary War.

Pennypacker, like Turn, and many writers who have written about the Culper Ring thereafter, have deviated from the truth in their accounts of the ring's history. The absence of footnotes in Pennypacker's works led some readers to mistake anecdotes and urban legends for verifiable facts. Unfortunately, many other authors have just rehashed these claims without providing any supporting evidence or analysis. They may have even gone to Long Island historians who have dedicated their careers to the study of the topic, but historians' advice wasn't always taken.

Long Islander and Fox News co-host Brian Kilmeade is the genre's most famous author. Together with Don Yaeger and other authors, he had meetings with local historians from Culper-related communities, including Setauket and Oyster Bay, to prepare for their 2013 hit. They gave him a lot of data, but he chose to disregard what didn't match his story. He also crossed over into historical fiction by peppering the work with made-up conversations between characters without making clear that they never really happened.

Alexander Rose re-examined the data for his 2006 book Washington's Spies, finding fault with several of Pennypacker's inferences but validating the fundamental work of Woodhull, Townsend, Roe, Brewster, and their friends. Both A Peculiar Service (1965) by Corey Ford and George Washington's Secret Six (2013) by Brian Kilmeade and Don Yaeger is presented as factual descriptions of the Culpers while using substantial fictitious sequences and language.

There are still historical puzzles and arguments surrounding the Culper Ring. The intricacies of how the Culper Spy Ring functioned will continue to captivate historians and history fans, but lacking fresh findings, many of the issues will stay unsolved.

Chapter Eleven
Conclusion

The American Revolutionary War was finally won in 1783. The 13 colonies under British rule were now the sovereign nation called the United States of America. Although tens of thousands of brave Americans served their country throughout the seven-year conflict, history has all but forgotten a select few.

The name given to the group was the "Culper Spy Ring." General George Washington's spy network worked in and around New York City for five years without being detected by the British. Members of the ring were aware of the consequences of being exposed. Captain Nathan Hale was killed during Washington's first effort to plant a spy on Long Island.

Hale was a teacher and a Yale University alum. The man volunteered for espionage work despite his lack of experience. The assignment Hale was on to provide crucial data to his superior commander was a failure. He volunteered for the mission, and only two weeks later, he was dead, having been hung by the British for espionage. For many days, the corpse of Hale was kept hanging as a warning to any other potential informants. He was laid to rest in a cemetery with no headstone.

Washington was profoundly affected by Hale's death. After realizing that he couldn't gather all the military data he needed, he assembled a team. An organization of spies was just what he needed. As a result of the Culper Ring's efforts, the Continental Army had a better understanding of the capabilities and potential intentions of the British military.

Many memorials of Nathan Hale's bravery and sacrifice have been created throughout the years. Several places in the United States and New York carry his name: educational institutions from kindergarten through college, a town in New York, a military base in Germany, a submarine in the United States Navy, and a fort from the Revolutionary War. In 1985, Hale was formally honored as Connecticut's state hero.

So yet, however, no Culper Spy Ring members have been memorialized in the form of sculptures. They should be honored right along with the many other Revolutionary War heroes. For their new homeland, the Culper Spy Ring, led by Tallmadge, were willing to sacrifice all in a war that many thought was hopeless. After all, they were fighting one of the world's most formidable armies, the British Army.

Is there anything we can learn from Washington's spies now? This is the lesson of humility. They looked out for one another by not discussing good or bad conflicts with anybody else. They never shared their secrets with anybody else again. It's a lesson we can all take away from it, and maybe that's the finest epitaph we can give them in this "Look at Me - Tell All" age of social media.

Chapter Twelve

"Discuss with Friends and Family"

Discussion Question

Lieutenant Caleb Brewster of Norwalk, Connecticut, approached Washington in August 1778 and offered his services as an intelligence source. What is the significance of intelligence sources in terms of warfare? Is it acceptable to spy on one's enemy? Why do you say so?

Discussion Question

With the help of Tallmadge, Washington tasked General Charles Scott with dealing with Brewster and finding other operatives. What, in your opinion, are the benefits of a network of spies? What do you believe are its drawbacks?

Discussion Question

While Tallmadge advocated for embedding operatives and maintaining a safe channel of contact, Scott supported sending out agents on one-off missions and having them report back to base afterward. Which of the two strategies do you favor? Why do you favor this strategy?

Discussion Question

After getting Scott's blessing, Tallmadge came up with a list of aliases for the major participants. How effective are the spies' aliases in concealing their identities? What benefit did this provide to the Culper Spy Ring?

Discussion Question

It is widely assumed that Washington came up with the moniker "Culper" for the network. How did he coin the term "culper"? When did the general population become aware of the espionage network?

Discussion Question

As the conflict carried on, security was strengthened by replacing numbers for people, places, and things. Why must they boost security while the battle continues? If you were one of the spies, what tactic would you recommend to your colleagues?

Discussion Question

The extent to which publisher James Rivington was involved in the espionage ring is a point of contention among historians. Who exactly is James Rivington? What was his alleged involvement inside the espionage network?

Discussion Question

Even though a generic female is only referenced once in the letters, Agent 355 is presumed to have been a female Culper operator. Who do you believe to be Agent 355? What makes you think she's Agent 355?

Chapter Thirteen

"Test Your Knowledge"

Quiz Question

1. **True or False:** Woodhull visited New York City to collect information. Mary Underhill, his married sister, resided there, so he visited. On October 31, 1778, he was questioned at a British checkpoint, which raised his uneasiness about the mission, but he returned to Setauket with crucial intelligence regarding the British supply ships.

2. **True or False:** Woodhull had to return to Setauket to convey messages to Caleb Brewster and receive communications from Tallmadge via Brewster. Tallmadge set up messengers in December to run the 55 miles between New York and Setauket, first Jonas Hawkins and then Austin Roe. The courier's job was to deliver letters to Brewster, who would convey them across Long Island Sound with his whaleboat crews to Tallmadge in Fairfield, Connecticut.

3. **True or False:** Anna Strong, a Setauket resident, and Abraham Woodhull's acquaintance and neighbor, allegedly helped pass along

spy ring communications by displaying preset signs. If she hung a black petticoat, Brewster had come in his whaleboat. She hung white handkerchiefs to show where he was hiding.

4. **True or False:** In June 1779, Woodhull sent Robert Townsend to New York City as "Samuel Culper Jr." Townsend had business there; thus, his trips raised less suspicion than Woodhull's. His tailoring company provided access to British officers.

5. **True or False:** Due to stringent secrecy, Washington didn't know all the agents' identities. Roe and Hawkins had to decipher Townsend's identity, but Woodhull wouldn't provide it. The Culper Ring employed coded signals and invisible ink, dubbed a sympathetic stain, to convey information.

6. **True or False:** George Washington sought to develop a spy network in New York City in 1777 after Nathan Hale's single operation. The Continental Army commander-in-chief hired Nathaniel Sackett, a merchant from Fishkill, to acquire information. Benjamin Tallmadge, a Yale graduate from Setauket, Long Island, was chosen as Sackett's military liaison.

7. **True or False:** Tallmadge updated the security system in 1779 by creating a "pocket dictionary" with an enlarged coding. The 710 terms picked were the most likely to be utilized. Each word was replaced by a number, such as "murder," by 387.

8. **True or False:** Hercules Mulligan revealed the British's intention to attack Washington on March 5, 1781. Mulligan was under suspicion and couldn't contact Washington directly, so he sent the information to Townsend, who delivered it through the Culper Ring. Washington received the message in time to evade the trap and take another way to the meeting.

Quiz Answer

1. True

2. True

3. True

4. True

5. True

6. True

7. True

8. True

Bonus Download

Want to Fill Your Digital Library for Free?

Every purchase comes with FREE bonus downloads! Download yours now by clicking the 'Get it Now' button.

Get it Now

Scan Your Phone to open QR code

Final Words From the Author...

Dear Reader,

    It was my utmost privilege performing a deep dive to bringing this book for you today.

Before saying goodbye, I'd like to take opportunity to offer you one final gift. If you've enjoyed this book, may I ask for a small review?

If you do, I'll send you for FREE a most cherished and valuable gift as a way of showing my utmost appreciation:

Bestsellers Top 7 Treasure Box

These are my personal bestsellers sold at bookstores valued at ~$30USD, my gift to you absolutely FREE.

To claim your gift:

1. Leave a review where the book was purchased
2. Send a screenshot to irvinepress@mail.com
3. Receive your gift of **Bestsellers Top 7 Treasure Box**

Sincerely,

History Encounters

THANK YOU

Table of Contents

Dedication

This poetry collection is dedicated to all of the important people in my life that have supported me and made my life worth living.

My children; Aidan, Braxton and Crystelle, all of you are my precious gems. When you eventually read this collection as adults, may it be a beacon to you to follow your own dreams wherever they may lead you. I love you.

My Stepmom and my Dad; Thank you Jennifer for supporting my writing and never losing faith in me no matter how long it took. Thank you Dad for everything, truly. When I was young, I never gave you the credit you deserved for being a great parent. I recognize and appreciate the work you put in a lot more now than I ever did.

Also my friends; Luna, Adri and Krystal (Quinn), Jessie (Sorina), Patrick (Topo), Caleb (Abaddon), Mike (Rhino), Lyra, Bat, John and Kiana (Destria) who have gotten me through some of the worst moments of my life and helped me to have fun in the midst of it. Knowing each and every one of you has made me a better person. You all deserve the world and a better one that we currently survive on. I hope to repay your kindness some day, this is a small start.

Luna, out of all of the people listed I've known you the longest and you've made me a better person just by knowing you. You inspire me in many ways that you don't even know about. You challenge me to think about things differently. I love you as if you were my own child and just like my own children, I hope to make you proud one day. I love working with you, it's one of the greatest joys of my life and I hope to work with you for many years to come.

Adri, some of this collection was written with you in mind as a muse, I hope you can see the good in yourself in its pages. I hope it serves to remind you of how wonderful you are. Thank you for everything you have been to me and hopefully will be. I adore you to the ends of the Earth and back.

Jessie, you have been an absolute rock for me over the years, I'm thankful to have you as a part of my life, as both a friend and adopted mother figure. You are such a joy to know and be around. You are someone I look up to, admire and respect so much, and always have.

Krystal, you didn't just walk into my life, you busted down the door and said "I'm here, mofo" in one of my darkest hours (I laughed as I wrote this and figured you'd appreciate the humor). You bring such warmth, light and laughter to my life, sometimes it hardly feels real after so much darkness. You are my sister for life and my love for you is unending.

I owe so much to each and every one of you for being patient, gentle and understanding with me in my worst moments. I hope I can one day repay your kindness and humbly thank you for being **my tribe**.

"The blood of the covenant is thicker than the water of the womb."

This collection of poetry is also dedicated to all other survivors of domestic violence, childhood trauma and sexual assault. May this collection be a reminder to you of your own power and justice for you. Never let yourself be silenced and go change the world.

Lastly, Resting Face and No are dedicated to all of those that are oppressed by the patriarchy. May we all keep finding our voices and busting down the doors of the past to create a new, better and brighter future for everyone.

Trigger Warning

This poetry collections contains references to: childhood trauma, narcissistic abuse, sexual assault, domestic violence, suicide, self harm, patriarchal oppression, war and explicit content.
It is not recommended for anyone under the age of 18 or anyone who would be triggered by these subjects.

Recovery

I am far more traumatized than
I ever let myself believe.
Believing the lies I told myself
that walls of protection
around me were recovery.
That I could control myself
into being healthy.

My whole world had to burn
and leave me standing alone
as the only remaining pillar
to recognize the match
was in my hand the whole time.
And simultaneously, that I
had finally taken the first real step.

Sorry Mom

Sorry Mom for not being
who you wanted me to be,
but I'm not sorry that I
became who I really am.
Sorry Mom that I didn't
live up to your expectations,
but I'm not sorry that I found me.
Sorry Mom that you saw
my self discovery as an act of rebellion,
but I'm not sorry for all
of the mistakes I made to find her.

Sorry Mom that I earned the title
"disappointment" but I'm not sorry
that I found my truth.
Sorry Mom that I let you down,
but I'm not sorry that I finally stepped
into my own power.
Sorry Mom that affection wasn't
your strength but I'm not
sorry that it's mine.

Sorry Mom that I learned
more on my own than I learned from you,
but I'm not sorry that I'm enlightened.
Sorry Mom that my newly
gained power triggered your entitlement
but I'm not sorry that I stood up for myself.
Sorry Mom that I didn't
remain meek when you stepped on me,
but I'm not sorry I rose from underneath.

But if you could just appreciate who I am
instead of mourning the idea of who you
wanted me to be,
I wouldn't have to keep saying sorry.

Heart of Glass

You were the first to
teach me I am second.
The first to put me last.
The first to sear
my soul to reckon,
the one who turned
my heart to glass.

You created this void,
for which there is no fill.
The first to teach me death
isn't the only thing that kills.

The love that I wanted,
was that which was denied.
My love wasn't valuable enough,
my childhood was the price.

You poached my adolescence as
much as the villain who stole my virtue.
Enabling him like an accomplice,
waiting for the escape cue.

I hate you for what you are,
for as many reasons as
the innumerable stars.
I hate that you've been so close,
but act as if I am incredibly far.
Maybe you could reach me,
if only you would try.
Love might yet be the cure,
while narcissism is the crime.

Your Villain

Make me your villain,
I promise I'll do it better.
Because my heart is full,
it's familiar with pain and pain
drives the greatest macabre.
Pain is just love's outcast,
just like me.

I would rather never have been born
than to be raised by a vulture.
Once upon a time,
my benevolence made me the most
trusted because unlike you
my tongue wasn't loose.
It wasn't in a constant rush to recite
news that should have burned
from the inside to utter.

My nature wasn't anchored in betrayal.
Every well earned secret was safe
under my guard.
When you skewered me through
the gut, you freed me from your
contract for fealty.
I owe no affection to those who
don't show any for me.
I'm free to release all of
what you concealed
into the world and let you clean
up your own misdeeds.

Family is only a word
when not proven.
What is chosen is stronger
than what is forced.
Blood of the covenant
is greater than the water

of the womb.
I don't owe you more
than I ever got.
It was you who perpetuated
villainy when you
siphoned love from us.
Your love is a crucifix that
expects self sacrifice
to your open hand.
You only ask for everything
with nothing in exchange.

Make me your villain and I will
take the cauldron where you
mix your poison and bathe you
in all of your worst fears.

You will swallow a dish of hypocrisy
made with your own entitlement
while I watch you choke on it.

You won't see the storm cloud of
your own creation until it descends,
clears everything in its path
and everyone has become an enemy.
Your life will disintegrate into nothing
as a cautionary tale passed through
the ages as an example
of what love is not.

Supply

My head is swimming,
but who's there?
Who understands,
who actually cares?
The vigilant friend
sits on the bottom
notch of the totem pole,
the last to receive in line.

When manic and anxiety visit,
no one recognizes the signs.
In the vault of compassion,
empathy's currency wanes.

Who is responsible for
loving this person?
No one.
When the need arises,
all voices turn to each other
and answer "no one".

"Not I, not them."

In accordance to their needs,
their expectations must be met.
The same of me isn't said.
"Busy," "Have no time,"
"Too much in my head",
to just be a friend,
all the while picking and choosing,
who deserves time.

When the supply runs out,
the reasons to stay all leave.

Strong

I am strong because I wanted to be.
I made a decision that I wasn't going to accept the least.
I am strong because I was raised by a woman who wasn't.
I looked in the mirror and decided
that I never wanted to repeat her mistakes.

I am strong because I had to be.
I had people depending on me
to give them a better example and
liberate them from misery.

I am strong because life gave me wars.
I played the hand that I was dealt,
and busted down doors.

I am strong because I chose to teach
myself what I didn't know.
I didn't come equipped,
so I sought to educate myself.
I am strong because despite all of that,
I can still love freely.
I am still soft at heart and
pain has not hardened me.

My Love

My love is different.
My love doesn't have
wings on its feet.
My love won't leave because of
angry words and difficult truths,
whether mine or yours.

It's not bathed in loosely thrown words,
confusion riddled and lie torn.
My love doesn't taste selfish
but it is protective,
if not a little greedy.

My love is action over words.
My love doesn't tell you that
you have to accept the least.

The message of my love is not
that I am a loser who isn't willing
to be more than what I am,
nor rise to your level.
Instead my love is intentional,
certain and secure.
My love won't tell you
that you are less.

My love won't leave you in neglect.
My love will respect you, your needs, your space.
My love is honest with shortcomings.
My love is raw with humanity
but will work for better.
My love is learning,
but also growing.
My love is not perfect but
it will continue to try.

My love is consistently reliable.
My love is rooted in the darkness
so it's prepared to conquer your monsters.

LIPS OPEN

My love is full of forgiveness.
My love won't put your needs last.
My love will lead you to be your best.
All that my love wants, is you, wholly, only,
with as much exclusivity as it will show you.
My love only requires you to bring all of yourself,
give all of yourself as it will give to you.

Feet of Flight

Your feet carry you away,
from anything that smells
like responsibility.
Like wings that sprout
from your ankles,
you seamlessly dodge accountability.

Leaving in your wake
a wild fire of broken hearts
and unanswered questions.

Woe for those who
dare to love you.
Those who are seduced
by your shallow charm
that hides your
roaring insecurities.

A coward in the face
of the pain you inflict.
Bravery is not just for those
who take up the sword,
but also those who arm
themselves with their heart.

Anarchy

Hate is a burden,
but love is a cross.
Aggression is a weight,
but passivity is a crutch.
Fury is a weapon,
but peace is a shield.

Velleity is a crime,
but reason is a sentence.
Passion is a noose,
but reserve is a void.
Fidelity is an anchor,
but treachery is an infinity.

Hope is a burn,
but pessimism is a cage.

Love for Toxicity

She'll open the skies for the heights of your ego.
She'll paint the clouds with
compliments for you.
She'll make you believe in
the power of transformation.
She'll make shrines out of your name.
She'll make fire rain on your enemies
with the depths of her loyalty.

Her defense of you could shatter
the gates of Hell.
She'll convince you the world is yours
with the confidence she inspires.
She will break through a dam
of insults for your honor.
She will bomb you with love that makes you blind.
Until she shows you her love is just a fable,
and her answer to responsibility is simply to deny.

Little Lies

When I see you now,
all respect is gone.
Your smiles are plastic.
It's tape that holds them on.
Your whole lives,
are little lies.
Your agenda intricately moves you
from one crowd to the next.

Friendships bound by
threads of dependency.
Treacherous as wolves
of the timber.
False love,
ingenuine loyalty,
disguised whispers,
shallow depths are
all that you truly share.

Enough toxicity between
you to be nuclear.
Smoking feet burn wooden planks
behind steps without consequence.
Where will you run when
the final match falls?
When you try to return
only to find the bridge is rotten?

Aftermath

Anxious mind, rabid heart.
Monstrous in their needs.
Caged in their impart.
Failing in their reach.
Do you trust only in
what you can see?

The eyes won't tell you
the heart feels sliced by a blade.
The eyes won't see that the weapon
is words and resounds with a sharper edge.

The eyes won't see the fabric
of her identity unraveling.
The eyes won't see the details
of her struggle.

The eyes won't notice
the war in her chest.

The eyes will mask her
fragile self esteem.
The eyes will hide
love's cry.
The eyes will bury
heart's greed.

Safety

I want to have the right words
when you need them.
I want to have the eyes
that memorize every detail.
I want to have the strength
you need when emotions are difficult.
I want to have the arms
that are the fortress that protects you.
I want to have the feet
that stay firmly planted during the storms.

I want to be the pillow
where you rest your head.
I want to have the mind
that keeps you captivated.
I want to be the net
that catches you when you fall.
I want to have the heart
that knows you as well as it does itself.
I want to have the reassurance
you need that you're safe.
Your body is safe, your mind is safe,
your heart is safe, your soul is safe,
those you love are safe...
.....with me.

MARS SAINT

The Entrant Dance

Exoneration is a bill I can't afford.
The cost has been too steep.
Caged petulance afflicts my core.
My mind lays in waste.
My heart is an empathetic heap.

Yet the bite of affinity continues its plague.
You broach peace,
but the memory steals my days.

Will a night come that I am free?
No longer held as an inmate?
Where the moon is not my only company?
Or will I be my own defeat?

Will this war riddled bout be my only embrace?
Or will serenity and I finally meet?
No, I'm too adrift to be saved.
The weight of ire grows heavy.
For me, it is too late.
I feel myself shredding.
Splintered, unhinging at all seams.
Take the path where salvation is paved.
Get out now, while your break is clean.

Yes, I Asked For It

Yes, I asked for it.
I asked for it in an evening conversation,
warped by naivety.

I asked for it in your conniving voice
lacing together lies of a dying marriage,
begging for sympathy.

I asked for it in the steps taken
to another room to conceal your treachery.

I asked for it in the moonlit
shadows of chosen family.

I asked for it in the solid enclosure
that barred me from escaping.

I asked for it in the strength of a hand
that hindered my militancy.

I asked for it in the clawed lead to the inguinal.
I asked for it in the fear that
reflected demonic qualities back at me.

I asked for it for the sake of children,
who were at your mercy.

I asked for it in the dull fog of a lagoon,
in propositions for secrecy.

I asked for it in a empyrean nook,
where marital vows laced an eternal boundary.

I asked for it with a sweaty palm
jarring a truck door for rampancy.

I asked for it in the glow of illuminated
pane, cornered in the crook of solidity.

I asked for it in the anguish of insomniac recreancy.
I asked for it in starvation's potency.
I asked for it in lucid nightmares rupturing
sleep's consistency.
I asked for it in the ache of physical apathy.
.....Yes, I asked for it.

A Heart Turned Hard

A life of innocence,
swept through the world's cruelty.
What once was pure became bitter.
Eyes that once were oblivious to fault,
was beaten by sharp tongues
and mercilessly pointing fingers.

Forgiveness freely given,
became a double edged sword,
relentlessly cutting its holder.

A heart, starving.
Left in hunger.
Abandonment.
Shame.
Abuse.
Neglect.

They all became regular occurrences.
Knives that repeatedly drove their blade
of perdition into repentant flesh.
Knees fallen in groveling weep for mercy
she afforded others, denied the one in need.

Penance became her own idol.
Her remedy for a cureless disease.
An addiction.
A coping mechanism.
An endless search for approval,
acceptance turned the remedy into affliction.

Pieces gradually chipped away,
until an abyss was all that remained of her.
A heart bled empty of every altruistic emotion.
The slowest death of a soul.

Could you hear the cries of anxiety?

No because your ears were deaf to her.
What was soft turned hard.
Sweet became morose.
Vibrant, turned obsidian.
A shell of protection encompassed.
She was the most dangerous of all
because she had nothing left to lose.

Support

Can I tell you what I'm thinking?
Will you care about what I say?
Can I show you what burns
the brightest in my heart
and feel in return that you
have caught the spark?

Will you tell everyone about
my light between heaven and hell?
Will the light become your flag
you carry to call a tribe
to spread the light?

Will you be the fan that makes
the light a flame?
Will you think of me?
Can you give what
you don't need?

Gratitude

Love may be fickle but it is also blind,
yet one thing life cannot be without.
To live is to love.

Love for yourself as well as love
for the opportunity to just be.
To experience all the wonders of the world
and all the secret desires we never profess.

A life without love is an empty shell
of an existence.
Mundane in its repetitive cycles.

Love is dancing in the rain,
communicating without words,
laughing at inappropriate times,
sneaking out together,
random affection and endearments.

Love is spontaneity.
Love is freedom.

Seal of Life

Nothing and no one can save me.
I loved with a rich abandon.
I excrete altruism until I was dry.
I choked on my own redemption.
I swallowed words that tasted like Hell.
Fear was the sword I pierced
gentle hearts with.
The cost to me was greater
than the size of the universe.
No one can save me.
No one...
But maybe, him.

Abnegation

It feels like suffocating when I say what I need.
I'll stutter, let my eyes burn holes in the floor,
squeeze nails into my palms until they bleed.

I can remember so many times before,
the words felt like sandpaper against my tongue
when they spilled into the air.
I remember when what I received,
for letting them free,
was screams like banshees.
Lips that spit knives through my skin,
feet that kicked dirt in my eyes as they started to leave.

What I fear even more,
is the self-centered way I feel.
How do you ask for something
you don't feel right asking for?
Worse still, how do you ask for
what you don't feel you deserve?

Yet, that feeling of being loved is an elusive yearning.
Something like a distant star in an
obscure sky, out of reach.

My thoughts gnaw on the stem of my mind
with jagged little teeth.
They won't let me forget.
They won't give me peace.

I just want to feel loved,
somewhere other than my dreams.

All A Dream

Please don't tell me
this was all a dream.
Don't tell me that
you've decided to leave.
Don't break my heart
into pieces.

Don't lie to me about
what you feel.
Don't hide from me.

My heart's on my sleeve
but I'm keeping it sheathed
until you return to me.

If you don't,
I don't know what I'll be.
I don't want to be free.
I don't want to lose how
you make me feel.

I know what exists is real.
Don't try to convince me
That it's all just a dream.

Religion

Your love is a disguise you use
to conceal decay like rotting flesh
and the hole where a soul never grew.
A flag you wave for society
yet you don't stand for its meaning
because it's one you don't understand.

Love never breached the surface,
you made it nothing but a performance.
Appearance is everything
to those who have nothing underneath.
When that appearance is
shallow, you won't get any deeper.
The thing about disguises though,
they always fall off.

Finally Safe

You are home and I am a hermit.
Air returned to my lungs when
I became yours again.

With you I am seen.
I am heard.
I am understood.
I am safe.

Anxiety isn't riddling my every thought
and decision when I am around you.
I don't feel eggshells splintering
through my words.

You bathe me in freedom
and nurture me in belonging.
Love is the river in our veins
that quenches us.
It restores and empowers us
without condition.

Every side of me is safe in your arms.
I am the most myself with you.
Fear abandons me like the enemy it is,
because you are my shield.

Give Me Forever

The dance of your eyes awaken my soul.
They give me fire to live, to overcome the impossible.
They give me hope and joy.

Before you, I was tormented.
You gave me what none other could.
You are the very air in my lungs.
I would give that
to have my arms around you again.
To hear you tell me you love me.
To know you mean it and are mine forever.

To hear you'll stay, I would fight off anyone
that would threaten you.
Give me forever, and I'll spend it earning you everyday.
I might be able to survive, but life without you is incomplete.

Essence of Shadow

I'm only a shadow.
Glittering light
swallows me.

Veil of comfort
outshined by
interim rays of sun.

I fade onto the walls.
Denizens don't notice.
I'm a blanket of invisibility,
easily missed, never seen.
Crowds file inward,
while I skirt the sidelines.
Their voices carry like bells,
mine is obscured,
grinding for reception,
like sandpaper against
a wooden surface.

I am snuffed by neglect.
I will wither.
They will bloom.

Unsung Love

When did emotions rise,
like demons emerging
from Hell?
Where did the ache
begin that was tumultuous
like an angel fell?
How did these feelings
swallow me like the
might of a typhoon?

Why did I let you devour
me like prey consumed?
Who are you to gorge
on my heart?
To pretend that you didn't
allow us to fall apart?

To assume that my love
ever had an end?
To awaken hope you
never planned to tend?
To make me fall for you
all over again?

My Own Prison

I feel trapped and secluded.
I feel weak and sedated.
I feel dizzy and suffocated,
and I can't stop it at all.

I know it is my fault
that's how I was taught
that I am always wrong
I just want to be gone
I'm in my own prison.

There's nowhere to run,
nowhere to hide.
I clench this gun,
they ignore my screaming help cry,
I appear sane,
but I want to run away.
I'm about to break,
what kills me is the ache
For more than I can have.

I feel lost and confused,
there's too much abuse,
No one understand what I've been through,
the only sign is the bruise.

No

No I won't come to your bed
as a filler for your wandering hands.
No, I don't want your touch because it's just
the harbinger of your infidelity.
No, I don't want your body in contact with mine
because you've failed to caress my mind.

No I won't accept your derogatory compliments as flirtation.
No, I don't want back door arrangements as a substitute for romance.
No, I won't lower my standards to boost your ego.

No, I won't be quiet so you can continue to be complacent.
No, I won't stop shouting your guilt
until it takes form and splinters from my neck.

No, I won't stroke your vanity.
No, I won't be compliant.
No, I won't simply bend the knee.
No, I won't be an accomplice to entitlement.
No, I won't teach you all that you aren't owed.

No, I won't conform to your schedule.
No, I don't have to listen to you.
No, the purpose of my existence is
not to entertain you.
No I won't continue to undercut my
self esteem to raise yours.

Hunter

I am the Hunter.
My pain nourishes my hunger.
Angst replenishes my hate.
I need nothing and
no one but my own.
I am merciless.
Vengeful.
Savage.

I am the embodiment of darkness.
The one you fear the most.

Please

When the world is too much,
and you feel out of touch,
Please just remember,
I will always be here.
When the light turns to dark,
and you can't get too far.
Please just remember,
I will always be near.

When the road is filled with promises,
and no ground in between.
When you're feeling like you're all alone,
and you don't know what they mean.
Just close your eyes and cross your heart,
I will help you see.
Show you what real love can be.
If you please just remember,
I will always be here.

When the shadows appear,
I will chase away your fears.
Please just remember,
I will always be here.
When you just want to die,
and life's making you cry.
Please just remember,
I will always be near.

When the night gets too long,
and you just can't hold on.
Please just remember,
I will always be here.

When every other love is untrue,
don't forget I will always love you.
If you please just remember,
I will always be here.

When life tries to get you down,
you can come to me.
I may not mean much at all,
but I will set you free.

Trust your heart and
don't give in.
You're better than you think.
And when it all seems too much
to take you will always have me.

I will show you what true love is.
If you can please just remember,
I will always be here with you.

Reckless Words

Reckless words string
through my head,
spoken from mouths claiming love.
Love is divine,
on their receiving end,
but to me,
it's yelling,
reprimand,
threats from anger,
abandonment,
anxiety ridden.

They don't see the affects.
They don't notice the fear.
Erasers can't clean a harsh word's bite.

They don't comprehend,
They don't understand
their criticism branded me for life.
The scattered thoughts,
racing heart,
patterns become neurotic.
I can't let go,
I won't let go,
hands cling for life,
lungs refuse to breathe,
terrified they'll leave.

It's a difficult feat to love me.
The next thing, their backs will be all I'll see.

Garden of Eden

I want a lifetime to use
your title in beg of ardor.
Put a flower in my hair,
for every time you show you care.
Watch the beauty grow,
as the vines entwine
and wind down my spine.

Climb the ladder of my rib cage,
and kiss your way back down.
I want a lifetime of hearing
my name burned into your lips.

See how the gold falls,
as the seasons pull me into light;
galaxy brown in my eyes,
as warm as skin to skin,
the garden grows, I am the bed.
I need the commanding undertone
it takes when it asserts love.

Pull me into the dark with ease
and I shall be my own light.
I shall fight my own fright.
I want forever to hear your growls,
sing the ode of passion against my ear.
I'd love nothing more than a life
full of the lull of your voice.

So long as the touch of your flowers
do stay, I'll live
and I'll grow, hence forth,
each and every day.

Person of Interest

I am beheld but omitted.
A listless mystery.
An awkward fit.
My depths reach measures
of infinity,
that no person aspires to reach.

The facets of my being,
no one's interest piqued.
A heart can ache,
more than romance one can seek.

Connection, the epitome
of existence.
Devoid of, leaves its victim
in havoc's wreak.
Towers of the heart
built for safety's defenses.
Many arms available,
but none that reaches.

How did I become transparent?
Where is the paint that disguised
what makes me aberrant?
Why are my shades not vibrant?
Are my flavors stale?
What is my defect?

I'm an imposition on others' solace,
leaden to their hearts.
The pursuit is only a
campaign of taunt.
I bow to defeat,
conclusion arrives,
a person of interest
will never be me.

When

When did it begin to feel like you stole the air from my lungs?
When did you narrow my vision to only seek you?
When did I become like a pile of glass without you?
When did the utterance of your name begin to excite my lips?

When did need overwhelm my existence?
When did the Heavens shine its brilliance on me
and decide to bestow this blessing?
When did I deserve this gift?

When did my stone spine turn to clay?
When did you become my nourishment?
When did you create my peace?
When did I relinquish myself with abandon to you?

When did you mark me as yours with a white hot brand?
When was the shift that turned comfort into passion?
When did stable love become irrevocably amorous?
When did you choose me as your forever?

War Zone

Every word I want to say,
that I want to seal in ink
is a prisoner of my mind.
The pen quivers in my hand.
Eloquent thoughts,
lapses to the heart in
the second of truth.

The mind fails in fluster,
the outpour similar to
a rushing waterfall dries up,
weak to the mind's clutter.

Mindset in frantic,
nerves fumbling.
Can I do anything right?
Mind and heart have gone to war
and I am the casualty.
I watched logic sacrifice
itself for the mind's campaign.
Heart claimed the victory.

Yet, their script abandon me
when they are most essential.

No One's Person

The mirror doesn't lie.
The mirror subjects me
to a truth I cannot deny.
Inside its double panes
I am vilified.
There's no other but
me myself and I.

I am me.
I am singular.
Singularity means alone.
Alone is the enemy,
yet also the friend.

Like a cave that shields
as much as swallows.
I am no one's person
like those of everyone.

Someone they wouldn't
trade for anyone.
No one to cherish
until life expires.
No one to embellish
share victorious praise.
I am not made for priority.

Only a ghost to
sojourn the conclave.
I am the presence
behind the wall of glass,
the unsung phantom
of the soiree'.

Yours

No amount of time with you can be enough.
Hours pass far too fast.
Before we know it,
we've been wrapped in each other for months.

But we're not a fly by night.
We're the eternal,
staying kind.
We're the type of love
that will last the ages.
We're the kind people
will look and envy.
You're the one my soul
has cried for.

Your love feeds me
all the way to the core.
To you I am bound
by every stitch
of flesh and spirit.

Never could a creature walk
the earth and be as exquisite.
How could such profound beauty,
brilliant mind
and divine personality
be wrapped in one?
Truly a gift sent
to me from above.

For all the days
of my life,
every breath is
breathed for you.
My bleeding heart,
is where your name
is tattooed.

Kill Me

Kill me with your silence.
Watch my cries leak from my veins.
Destroy me with your neglect.
See the crack in my heart when it's dead.
Bury me in your indifference.
Notice my body become a cold, hardened shell.
Ignore my pleads for your love.
Watch my soul carried on a cloud above.
Disregard my suffering,
until it's lying lifeless at your feet.
Know me not in life,
deny me while I'm alive.
Only to gain sympathy when I die.
Forget my existence while there's time.
But when I'm boxed in Earth's eternal bed,
don't mourn then, for what you never said.
Don't wear a shroud of pain,
for what wasn't felt each time I forgave.

Heartbeat

You were the shadow in my mind,
that I could never forget.
The beast who was always gentle
with me no matter what was outwardly believed.

Our souls intertwined even in the early days
and brought us to meet on another level where
a foundation of friendship and
respect could build a love that was divine.

It was us that always protected one another.
You were always lurking to defend me.
We grew to know one another at our essence.

Through even the worst of ourselves,
it was always us.
We were a match.
A meeting of fire and steel
that forged greater strength in us.

An invisible string pulling us to a greater destiny.
When our paths were prepared for one another
they finally intersected to create
a beautiful journey meant for only us.

Fear clouded the distance but couldn't
separate us even in the fog.
The solidarity of our bond mounted
and drew us to one another again.
A reunion of two hearts bound as one.

Love Has Never Been

All that I know of love is what love has never been.

Love has never been soft touches that pamper my skin.
Love has never been reassurances when the ghosts of trauma visit.
Love has never been peaked ears that are sensitive to my pain.

Love has never been observant to my needs without words.
Love has never been security that their eyes rest only on me.
Love has never been bright eyes that understand my hesitation.
Love has never been romantic gestures and words of flirtation.
Love has never been feisty hands that fight for my protection.
Love has never been a place I could rest and fall apart.
Love has never been somewhere I can remove my armor.

Love has never been where my flaws could show.
Love has never been acceptance of me as any other than perfect.
Love has never been the home where I'm not punished.
Love has never come without a cost.
Love has never been without conditions.
Love has never not wandered away for a better offer.
Love has never been a sanctuary for peace.
Love has never not sliced through me with criticisms.

But that's exactly what I want it to be.

Who Am I?

With a scar where my given name once was,
and a name I gave myself,
who am I?

With a revolving mind of interests,
and an ocean worth of dreams,
who am I?

With emotions that decide my gender,
and my whole life split in two,
who am I?

With a desire to be good,
and an affinity for darkness,
who am I?

With a drive to love,
and a repulsion to be loved,
who am I?

With emotions on overdrive,
and an expression blank as paper,
who am I?

With laughter that seeps through my pores,
and a fortress around my emotions,
who am I?

With a yearning to connect,
and a malady that prevents connection,
who am I?

With a penchant to be vulnerable,
and a blockage that prevents vulnerability,
who am I?

Resting Face

The rest in my face is anything but restful
when rebuke has licked the self esteem
from its surface.

When war has spit flames that scorched
the flesh until it withered and transformed
into the countenance of a black widow.

When survival was the ruler that
commanded an army of resilience.
Under the surface of rest, emotion boils.
A festering anarchy that edges the lips
and has finally found a home on the face
of someone who is tired of injustice.

Protest is mapped in the streams of a mouth
that remains consistently ready to bite off
the hand that has commanded
her to be compliant.

Rest is a disguise to replace acquiescence that,
once upon a time, was conditioned obedience.
As soon as a voice is raised in riot,
to speak above a volume of meek
and inclined to assertion,
is when the brand of the resting face,
is assigned, as if it were a scarlet letter.
Once you cease to accommodate oppressors,
you receive the nails of crucifixion.

As soon as you oppose, you become
the demon that crawled from a fissure
in the earth to drive men to extinction.
Their definition of respect is only
in exchange for the benefit of you.
They don't want your resting face.

Your resting face is a badge of honor
they want you to be ashamed of so
they never have to lift their boot off of your cheek,
and they never have to notice the boot
print left behind.

About the Author

Mars Saint is a mother of three amazing kids who are the light of her life, a friend to several equally wonderful people and enjoys life living in San Antonio, Texas, although she originated from Indiana and Ohio. When not writing, Mars can be found gaming, video editing, researching, studying astrology and hanging out with her family.